MW00900111

THIS NOTEBOOK
BELONGS TO : ____________________

Made in the USA
Monee, IL
28 July 2021

74500830R00056